THE SWISS RIVIERA

Exploring the Beauty of Lake Geneva

Moon M. Michael

The information contained in this book is for general informational purposes only. While we endeavor to keep the information up to date and correct, we make no representations or warranties of any kind, express or implied, about the completeness, accuracy, reliability, suitability, or availability concerning the book or the information, products, services, or related graphics contained in the book for any purpose. Any reliance you place on such information is therefore strictly at your own risk. In no event will we be liable for any loss or damage including without limitation, indirect or consequential loss or damage, or any loss or damage whatsoever arising from loss of data or profits arising out of, or in connection with, the use of this book?

Table of Content

Introduction

As I stepped off the train onto the platform at Montreux, the warm sun and gentle breeze welcomed me to the Swiss Riviera. I had always heard about the stunning beauty of Lake Geneva and the charming towns that surrounded it, but experiencing it firsthand was something else entirely.

As I walked along the lakeside promenade, I was struck by the stunning views of the shimmering lake and the soaring peaks of the Alps in the distance. The air was filled with the fragrance of blooming flowers and freshly brewed coffee from the sidewalk cafes.

As I explored the towns of Montreux, Vevey, and Lausanne, I was enchanted by their unique personalities and charming architecture. From the grand Chateau de Chillon to the quirky Charlie Chaplin Museum, there was always something new and exciting to discover.

But it was on the lake itself that I truly felt like I was experiencing the magic of the Swiss Riviera. Whether it was taking a leisurely boat tour or trying my hand at stand-up paddleboarding, being out on the water surrounded by stunning scenery was an experience I'll never forget.

"The Swiss Riviera: Exploring the Beauty of Lake Geneva" is a travel guidebook that takes you on a journey through one of the most picturesque regions of Switzerland. Nestled along the shores of Lake Geneva, the Swiss Riviera is a charming and vibrant destination that offers a unique blend of natural beauty, rich history, and modern amenities.

In this book, you'll discover the towns of Montreux, Vevey, and Lausanne, each with its distinct character and attractions. You'll explore must-see sights like the stunning Chateau de Chillon, the whimsical Charlie Chaplin Museum, and the fascinating Olympic Museum. You'll also learn about the exciting activities you can enjoy on the lake itself, such as boat tours, water sports, and scenic lakeside walks.

But this travel guide is more than just a list of attractions and activities. It also provides practical information on everything from when to go and where to stay, to tips for making the most of your trip. Whether you're a first-time visitor or a seasoned traveler, "The Swiss Riviera: Exploring the Beauty of Lake Geneva" is the perfect companion for anyone looking to experience the magic of this enchanting region.

About Lake Geneva

Lac Leman, also referred to as Lake Geneva in English, is a vast body of fresh water situated on the boundary separating Switzerland and France. It is the largest lake in Switzerland and one of the largest lakes in Western Europe, with a surface area of over 580 square kilometers. The lake is fed by several rivers, including the Rhone, and is surrounded by the majestic peaks of the

Alps, making for a breathtakingly beautiful backdrop.

Lake Geneva is not only a natural wonder but also a cultural and economic hub of the region. It is home to several charming towns and cities, including Montreux, Vevey, Lausanne, Geneva, and many more. The lake's shores are dotted with historic castles and museums, luxurious hotels, world-class restaurants, and vibrant nightlife venues. Lake Geneva also offers a variety of outdoor recreational opportunities, such as boating, fishing, swimming, hiking, and skiing in the nearby mountains.

Whether you're looking for a relaxing getaway, a romantic escape, or an adventurous vacation, Lake Geneva has something to offer everyone. Its natural beauty, rich history, and modern amenities make it a must-see destination for anyone visiting Switzerland.

Getting to the Swiss Riviera

Getting to the Swiss Riviera is easy, thanks to its central location and excellent transport connections. Here are a few options:

- **By plane:** The closest international airport to the Swiss Riviera is Geneva Airport, which is located just a short drive away from Montreux, Vevey, and Lausanne. The airport is served by several major airlines and offers direct flights from many cities around the world.

- **By train:** Switzerland has an extensive and efficient train network, and the Swiss Riviera is no exception. There are direct train connections from major Swiss cities such as Zurich, Bern, and Geneva to the towns of Montreux, Vevey, and Lausanne. The train journey from Zurich to Montreux takes around 2 hours and offers stunning views of the Swiss countryside along the way.

- By car: If you prefer to drive, the Swiss Riviera is easily accessible by car. The region is located at the intersection of several major highways, including the A9 and A1. However, keep in mind that parking can be a challenge in some of the towns, especially during peak tourist season.

- By boat: For a more scenic and leisurely option, you can also reach the Swiss Riviera by boat. Several boat tours operate on Lake Geneva, with stops in Montreux, Vevey, and Lausanne. This is a great way to take in the stunning views of the lake and the surrounding mountains while avoiding traffic congestion on the roads.

- No matter which mode of transportation you choose, getting to the Swiss Riviera is a breeze and the journey itself is a part of the experience.

Chapter 1
Exploring the Towns

Montreux

Montreux is a charming town located on the shores of Lake Geneva, in the heart of the Swiss Riviera. It is known for its mild climate, stunning scenery, and rich cultural heritage, making it a popular destination for tourists from around the world.

One of the main attractions in Montreux is the Chateau de Chillon, a medieval castle that dates back to the 12th century. The castle is one of the most visited historic sites in Switzerland and is known for its impressive architecture and beautiful location on a small island in the lake.

Montreux is also famous for its world-renowned jazz festival, which takes place every summer and attracts some of the biggest names in the music industry. The festival has been held annually since 1967 and has become a symbol of the town's cultural   identity.

In addition to the castle and the jazz festival, Montreux offers plenty of other attractions and activities for visitors to enjoy. These include taking a stroll along the scenic promenade, visiting the Freddie Mercury statue, exploring the old town with its charming streets and shops, and enjoying the local cuisine. You can dine in one of the numerous restaurants and cafes available.

Montreux is also a great base for exploring the surrounding area. The nearby mountains offer a range of outdoor activities, such as hiking, skiing, and snowboarding, while the nearby towns of Vevey and Lausanne offer even more cultural and historic sites to explore.

Montreux is a beautiful and charming town that offers a unique blend of natural beauty, cultural heritage, and modern amenities, making it a must-visit destination on any trip to Switzerland.

Vevey

Vevey is a picturesque town located on the northern shore of Lake Geneva, in the heart of the Swiss Riviera. Lausanne is renowned for its remarkable heritage, spectacular vistas, and lively cultural activities, which have contributed to its popularity among tourists from all over the globe.

One of the main attractions in Vevey is the **Alimentarium**, a museum dedicated to food and nutrition. The museum is located in a beautiful building on the lakefront and features interactive exhibits, educational workshops, and tastings. Visitors can learn about the history of food, the science of nutrition, and the cultural significance of food around the world.

Another popular attraction in Vevey is the **Charlie Chaplin statue,** a tribute to the legendary comedian who spent his later years in the

town. The statue is located in the town center and is a popular spot for taking photos and selfies.

Vevey is also known for its lively cultural scene, with numerous festivals and events taking place throughout the year. One of the most popular events is the Fête des Vignerons, a wine festival that takes place once every 20 years and celebrates the region's rich winemaking heritage.

In addition to the museum, the statue, and the festivals, Vevey offers plenty of other attractions and activities for visitors to enjoy. These include taking a stroll along the scenic lakefront promenade, exploring the charming old town with its narrow streets and historic buildings, and enjoying the local cuisine in one of the many restaurants and   cafes.

Overall, Vevey is a charming and vibrant town that offers a unique blend of history, culture, and natural beauty, making it a must-visit destination on any trip to Switzerland.

Lausanne

Situated on the bank of Lake Geneva, in the French-speaking part of Switzerland, Lausanne is a charming city known for its beauty. With its breathtaking landscapes, significant past, and lively cultural activities, it has become a favored location for visitors worldwide.

One of the main attractions in Lausanne is the **Olympic Museum,** a museum dedicated to the history and legacy of the Olympic Games. The museum is located in a beautiful building on the lakefront and features interactive exhibits, educational workshops, and a collection of Olympic artifacts and memorabilia.

The Cathedral of Notre Dame is another famous landmark in Lausanne, renowned for its exquisite Gothic architecture that originated in the 12th century. The cathedral is located in the heart of the old town and features impressive architecture, beautiful stained glass windows, and a panoramic view of the city from its tower.

Lausanne is also known for its lively cultural scene, with numerous festivals and events taking place throughout the year. One of the most popular events is the Lausanne Underground Film & Music Festival, a celebration of alternative cinema and music that takes place every October.

In addition to the museum, the cathedral, and the festivals, Lausanne offers plenty of other attractions and activities for visitors to enjoy. These include taking a stroll along the scenic lakefront promenade, exploring the charming old town with its narrow streets and historic buildings, and enjoying the local cuisine in one of the many restaurants and cafes.

Overall, Lausanne is a beautiful and vibrant

city that offers a unique blend of history, culture, and natural beauty, making it a must-visit destination on any trip to Switzerland.

Chapter 2
Must-See Attractions

Chateau de Chillon

Chateau de Cillon is a magnificent castle located in the beautiful countryside of the Swiss Canton of Vaud, near the town of Morges. The castle dates back to the 13th century and has been lovingly restored to its former glory, making it a popular destination for visitors who want to experience a piece of Swiss history.

One of the most unique details about Chateau de Cillon is its stunning architecture, which features a beautiful mix of medieval and Renaissance styles. The castle is made up of several buildings, including a main tower, a chapel, and a beautiful courtyard, all surrounded by a moat and gardens.

Inside the castle, visitors can explore a fascinating collection of medieval and Renaissance art and artifacts, including tapestries, furniture, and paintings. The castle also features a beautiful chapel with stunning stained glass windows, which are still used for weddings and other special events.

Another unique detail about Chateau de Cillon is its beautiful gardens, which are a popular spot for picnics and relaxation. The gardens feature a mix of formal and informal design elements, including beautiful flowers, hedges, and fountains, as well as a stunning view of the surrounding countryside.

Visitors to Chateau de Cillon can also enjoy a variety of activities and events throughout the year, including guided tours, medieval-themed events, and outdoor concerts. The castle is also a popular destination for weddings and other special events, with its beautiful gardens and historic charm providing the perfect backdrop for a memorable celebration.

Overall, Chateau de Cillon is a truly unique and beautiful destination in Switzerland, offering visitors a fascinating glimpse into the country's rich history and culture, as well as a peaceful retreat amid stunning natural beauty.

Charlie Chaplin Museum

The Charlie Chaplin Museum is a fascinating museum dedicated to the life and work of the legendary silent film star, Charlie Chaplin. The museum is located in the beautiful town of Vevey, on the shores of Lake Geneva in Switzerland, and is a popular destination for film lovers and history buffs.

One unique detail about the Charlie Chaplin Museum is its location in Chaplin's former home, a beautiful mansion called Manoir de Ban. The mansion was where Chaplin spent the last 25 years of his life, and it has been lovingly restored to its former glory to serve as a museum dedicated to his life and work.

Inside the museum, visitors can explore a range of exhibits and displays showcasing Chaplin's films, personal life, and artistic process. The museum features a vast collection of artifacts, including costumes, props, and memorabilia from Chaplin's films, as well as personal belongings such as letters, photographs, and home movies.

One of the most unique features of the Charlie Chaplin Museum is its interactive exhibits, which allow visitors to experience Chaplin's work in new and exciting ways. For example, visitors can try on costumes and perform in front of a green screen to recreate scenes from Chaplin's films or explore a recreation of the sets from his most famous movies.

In addition to the exhibits, the Charlie Chaplin Museum also features a beautiful restaurant and café, serving up delicious food and drinks inspired by Chaplin's life and films. The museum also hosts a range of events and activities throughout the year, including film screenings, workshops, and special exhibitions.

Overall, the Charlie Chaplin Museum is a unique and fascinating destination in Switzerland, offering visitors a chance to step into the world of one of the most iconic figures in film history and explore the life and work of this legendary artist in a beautiful and engaging setting.

Olympic Museum

The Olympic Museum is a world-renowned museum dedicated to the Olympic Games and the athletes who have competed in them throughout history. Located in the beautiful city of Lausanne, Switzerland, the museum is a must-visit destination for sports enthusiasts and anyone interested in the history of the Olympics.

One unique aspect of the Olympic Museum is its stunning location on the shores of Lake Geneva, providing visitors with beautiful views of the surrounding mountains and water. The museum is spread across three floors, each of which is packed with fascinating exhibits and displays that bring the history of the Olympics to life.

One of the most impressive features of the Olympic Museum is its vast collection of Olympic artifacts, which includes everything from medals and torches to uniforms and equipment used by athletes in the games. Tourists have the opportunity to delve into the history of the Olympics by examining these artifacts, gaining knowledge about the development of the games and the athletes who have participated in them throughout the   ages.

Another unique feature of the Olympic Museum is its interactive exhibits, which allow visitors to experience the excitement of the games firsthand. Visitors can test their skills in a range of sports, including running, swimming, and skiing, using state-of-the-art simulators and equipment. They can also explore the science of sports through interactive exhibits that teach about the physics and biomechanics of various Olympic   events.

The Olympic Museum also features a range of exhibits and displays dedicated to the culture and traditions of the Olympic Games, including art and music inspired by the games, as well as exhibits showcasing the host cities and countries that have played a role in the games over the years. In addition to the exhibits, the Olympic Museum also hosts a range of events and activities throughout the year, including workshops, lectures, and film screenings, as well as special exhibitions dedicated to specific sports or themes.

Overall, the Olympic Museum is a unique and fascinating destination in Switzerland, offering visitors a chance to explore the rich history and culture of the Olympic Games in a beautiful and engaging setting. Whether you're a sports enthusiast or simply interested in the history of the games, the Olympic Museum is a must-visit destination that will leave you inspired and awed.

Chapter 3

Activities on the Lake

Boat Tours

Boat tours in Switzerland are a popular way to explore the stunning scenery and landscapes of the country from a unique perspective. Many of Switzerland's lakes and rivers offer boat tours, providing visitors with an opportunity to see the country's natural beauty from the water.

One unique aspect of boat tours in Switzerland is the variety of experiences available. Visitors can choose from leisurely sightseeing tours to high-speed adventures and everything in between. Boat tours can range from short hour-long trips to full-day excursions, depending on the destination and the length of the tour.

During boat tours, visitors can expect to see some of Switzerland's most iconic landmarks and natural wonders, such as the stunning peaks of the Swiss Alps, picturesque villages and towns, and breathtaking lakes and rivers. Boat tours also provide a unique perspective on

Switzerland's architecture and culture, as many of the country's historic landmarks and buildings can be viewed from the water.

One of the most popular destinations for boat tours in Switzerland is Lake Geneva, where visitors can take a leisurely cruise around the lake, stopping at charming towns and villages along the way. Other popular destinations for boat tours in Switzerland include Lake Zurich, Lake Lucerne, and the Rhine River.

Boat tours in Switzerland also offer a range of amenities and services, depending on the tour company and the destination. Some tours may offer food and drinks on board, while others may provide audio guides or live commentary on the sights and landmarks along the way.

Overall, boat tours in Switzerland provide a unique and unforgettable way to experience the country's natural beauty and cultural landmarks. Whether you're looking for a leisurely sightseeing tour or an adrenaline-pumping adventure, a boat tour in Switzerland is a must-do activity for any traveler.

Water Sports

Water sports are a popular activity in Switzerland, particularly during the summer months when temperatures are warm and the lakes and rivers are inviting. There is a wide range of water sports activities available for visitors of all ages and skill levels, from relaxing boat rides to thrilling water sports adventures.

One of the most popular water sports activities in Switzerland is paddle boarding. Paddle boarding involves standing on a long board and using a paddle to navigate through the water. This activity can be enjoyed on lakes, rivers, and even in the sea, providing a unique and exciting way to explore Switzerland's waterways.

Kayaking and canoeing are also popular water sports in Switzerland. Visitors can rent a kayak or canoe and explore the country's lakes and rivers at their own pace. This is a great way to experience the country's natural beauty and wildlife up close and personal.

For those looking for a more thrilling water sports experience, Switzerland offers a range of options. Wakeboarding, water skiing, and windsurfing are just a few of the adrenaline-pumping activities available for visitors to enjoy. These sports are perfect for those looking for a challenge and a rush of excitement on the water.

Swimming and diving are also popular water activities in Switzerland. The country's clear and clean lakes provide excellent opportunities for swimming and diving, with many spots offering stunning views of the surrounding landscape.

In addition to these activities, visitors can also enjoy fishing, boating, and sailing on Switzerland's lakes and rivers. Whether you're looking for a relaxing day on the water or a thrilling adventure, there's something for everyone when it comes to water sports in Switzerland.

Lakeside Walks

Switzerland is home to some of the most stunning lakes in the world, and there's no better way to experience their natural beauty than by taking a lakeside walk.

Lakeside walks provide visitors with a unique opportunity to soak in the country's stunning landscapes, while also enjoying the fresh air and exercise.

One of the most popular lakeside walks in Switzerland is along the shores of Lake Geneva. The promenade in Montreux is particularly popular, offering stunning views  of the lake and the surrounding Alps. Visitors can stroll along the promenade, stopping to enjoy the various shops and restaurants along the way.

Lake Zurich also offers a scenic lakeside walk, stretching along the eastern shore of the lake. The walk takes visitors through charming villages and towns, with plenty of opportunities to stop and enjoy the view. On the opposite side of the lake, visitors can enjoy Zurichhorn Park, which offers a peaceful setting for a lakeside stroll.

Lake Lucerne is another popular destination for lakeside walks, with the stunning Swiss Alps towering in the distance. The path along the lake takes visitors through charming towns and villages, providing a unique perspective on the region's architecture and culture.

Other lakeside walks in Switzerland include

Lake Thun, Lake Brienz, and Lake Neuchatel. Each of these lakes offers a unique setting and stunning views, making them a must-  visit destination for any lakeside walk enthusiast.

Lakeside walks in Switzerland are suitable for visitors of all ages and fitness levels, with many paths offering a gentle and leisurely stroll. The walks are also accessible throughout the year, with different seasons providing a unique perspective on the country's natural beauty.

Overall, lakeside walks in Switzerland are a great way to experience the country's stunning landscapes and natural beauty, while also enjoying a peaceful and relaxing stroll.

Chapter 4

Nearby Excursions

Lavaux Vineyards

The Lavaux Vineyards is a stunning wine-growing region in Switzerland, located on the northern shores of Lake Geneva between Lausanne and Montreux. It is a UNESCO World Heritage Site and is known for its breathtaking terraced vineyards, which extend for over 800 hectares along the steep hillsides overlooking the lake.

The region is home to a unique microclimate, with the lake acting as a natural regulator of temperature and humidity. The combination of the region's soil, climate, and topography creates ideal growing conditions for a range of grape varieties, including Chasselas, Pinot Noir, and Gamay.

Visitors to the Lavaux Vineyards can enjoy a range of activities, including wine tastings, vineyard tours, and hikes through the stunning terraced landscapes. Many of the vineyards offer guided tours and tastings, providing visitors with the opportunity to learn about the region's history, winemaking techniques, and unique flavors.

The Lavaux Vineyards are also home to several charming villages and towns, including Saint-Saphorin, Epesses, and Lutry. These towns offer visitors the opportunity to explore the region's rich cultural heritage, with many historic buildings and churches dating back centuries.

Overall, the Lavaux Vineyards is a must-visit destination for wine enthusiasts and nature lovers alike. The region's stunning landscapes, rich cultural heritage, and world-class wines make it a unique and unforgettable destination in Switzerland.

Gruyeres Castle

Gruyeres Castle is a historic landmark located in the medieval town of Gruyeres in the Canton of Fribourg, Switzerland. The castle was built in the 13th century and has been preserved to this day as an important symbol of Swiss history and heritage.

Visitors to Gruyeres Castle can take a guided tour of the castle's interior, which features beautifully preserved rooms, furnishings, and artwork. The castle's architecture and decoration reflect the styles of different eras, ranging from Gothic to Renaissance.

One of the highlights of a visit to Gruyeres Castle is the opportunity to see the collections of the Gruyeres Museum, which is located within the castle walls. The museum showcases exhibits on the region's history and culture, including artifacts related to the castle's past.

In addition to the castle's historical significance, Gruyeres is also famous for its namesake cheese. Visitors to the town can enjoy a range of delicious dairy products, including cheese fondue, raclette, and Gruyeres cheese.

Beyond the castle, Gruyeres is a charming town with a medieval atmosphere, featuring narrow streets, traditional architecture, and stunning views of the surrounding countryside. Visitors can explore the town's shops, restaurants, and cafes, or take a stroll through the nearby hills and forests.

Overall, a visit to Gruyeres Castle is a must for anyone interested in Swiss history and culture. The castle's rich history, stunning architecture, and beautiful surroundings make it a unique and unforgettable destination in Switzerland.

Glacier 3000

Glacier 3000 is a popular tourist destination located in the Swiss Alps, near the town of Les Diablerets in the Canton of Vaud. The area is named after its altitude, as the glacier is located at 3,000 meters above sea level.

One of the main attractions at Glacier 3000 is the Peak Walk by Tissot, a suspension bridge that spans 107 meters and offers stunning views of the surrounding mountains and valleys. The bridge is the only one in the world that connects two mountain peaks.

Another popular activity at Glacier 3000 is skiing and snowboarding. The area features over 30 kilometers of slopes, with runs for all levels of experience. In addition, the glacier remains open for skiing and snowboarding even during the summer months.

For those looking for a more unique experience, Glacier 3000 also offers dog sled rides, snowshoeing, and ice climbing. Visitors can also take a ride on the Alpine

Coaster, a thrilling toboggan run that winds its way through the mountain terrain.

At the top of the glacier, visitors can enjoy stunning panoramic views of the surrounding landscape, including the Matterhorn and Mont Blanc. The area is also home to a range of restaurants and cafes, serving local cuisine and drinks.

In summary, Glacier 3000 is an essential place to visit for anyone seeking to witness the magnificence and thrill of the Swiss Alps. Its unique attractions, breathtaking scenery, and range of activities make it a destination that should not be missed.

Chapter 5

Dining and Nightlife

Local Cuisine

Switzerland is famous for its delicious and varied cuisine, which features a range of local and regional specialties. Each canton in Switzerland has its culinary traditions and specialties, making it a wonderful destination for food lovers.

One of the most famous Swiss dishes is **cheese fondue**, a hot and creamy cheese sauce made with Swiss cheese, white wine, and a touch of garlic. The fondue is typically served with bread cubes for dipping, making it a perfect winter comfort food.

Another popular Swiss dish is raclette, which is made by heating a wheel of cheese and scraping the melted cheese onto potatoes, meats, and vegetables. The dish is typically served with pickles, onions, and other accompaniments.

For meat lovers, Switzerland offers a range of delicious dishes, including the famous Zurich-style veal with creamy mushroom sauce, and the hearty and flavorful Swiss sausage known as cervelat.

In addition to these traditional dishes, Switzerland is also known for its chocolate and pastries. Visitors can indulge in a range of sweet treats, including the famous Swiss chocolate, creamy truffles, and fruit tarts.

Finally, no trip to Switzerland would be complete without trying some of the local wines. Switzerland produces a range of delicious wines, including the famous white wine from the Canton of Vaud, and the rich red wines from the Valais region.

Overall, Switzerland offers a rich and diverse culinary experience, with something to satisfy every taste and craving. Whether you are a fan of cheese, meat, chocolate, or wine, Switzerland is sure to delight your taste buds.

Best Restaurants

Switzerland is home to a wealth of fantastic restaurants, ranging from traditional Swiss eateries to international fine dining establishments. Here are just a few of the best restaurants that visitors to Switzerland should check out:

1. **Schloss Schauenstein** - located in the picturesque town of Fürstenau, this Michelin-starred restaurant is

renowned for its innovative cuisine and use of local ingredients.

2. **Restaurant de l'Hôtel de Ville** - situated in the town of Crissier, near Lausanne, this three-Michelin-starred restaurant is famous for its intricate and inventive dishes.

3. **Les Trois Rois** - located in the historic city of Basel, this elegant restaurant is known for its modern French cuisine and beautiful riverfront views.

4. **Stucki** - this Michelin-starred restaurant in Basel serves up delicious contemporary European cuisine, with a focus on locally-sourced ingredients.

5. **Restaurant Chesery** - located in the charming village of Gstaad, this popular restaurant serves up a range

of Swiss and international dishes, with an emphasis on seasonal ingredients.

6. **Zeughauskeller** - situated in the heart of Zurich, this historic restaurant is known for its traditional Swiss cuisine, including classic dishes like rosti and fondue.

7. **Kornhauskeller** - located in the historic city of Bern, this elegant restaurant is housed in a former granary and serves up delicious Swiss and European cuisine, with a focus on fresh and local ingredients.

These are just a few of the many fantastic restaurants that Switzerland has to offer. Whether you are looking for fine dining, traditional Swiss cuisine, or international flavors, Switzerland is sure to have a restaurant that will satisfy your taste buds.

Bars and Clubs

Switzerland offers a vibrant nightlife scene, with plenty of bars and clubs to suit all tastes and preferences. Here are some of the best bars and clubs in Switzerland that visitors should check out:

1. **Kaufleuten** - located in the heart of Zurich, this iconic nightclub features a range of musical genres and hosts international DJs and live performances.
2. **La Folie Douce** - situated in the popular ski resort of Verbier, this outdoor club is renowned for its lively

après-ski parties and stunning mountain views.

3. **Les Brasseurs** - located in Geneva, this popular microbrewery offers a range of delicious beers and hosts live music and events throughout the week.

4. **Bar 63** - situated in the heart of Basel, this stylish bar offers a range of classic and modern cocktails, as well as a great selection of wines and spirits.

5. **Cafe Bar Mokka** - located in the charming city of Thun, this popular bar and music venue offers a range of live music, comedy, and cabaret performances.

6. **El Lokal** - situated in the trendy Kreis 4 neighborhood of Zurich, this cozy

bar is known for its eclectic music scene and friendly atmosphere.

7. **Club Bonsoir** - located in the historic city of Bern, this popular nightclub offers a range of electronic music and hosts regular events and parties.

These are just a few of the many fantastic bars and clubs that Switzerland has to offer. Whether you are looking for a wild night out or a cozy spot to enjoy a drink with friends,  Switzerland is sure to have a spot that will meet your needs.

Chapter 6

Practical Information

When to visit

The ideal time to visit Switzerland mainly depends on your preferences for activities and sights during your journey. Here's a breakdown of the best time to visit Switzerland by season:

- **Winter (December - February):** This is the best time to visit Switzerland if you want to ski, snowboard, or enjoy other winter activities in the Swiss Alps. The peak season for skiing in Switzerland is from mid-December to mid-March, so expect higher prices during this time.

- **Spring (March-May):** Springtime in Switzerland is when the snow starts to melt, and flowers begin to bloom. This is a great time to visit if you want to avoid crowds and enjoy pleasant weather.

- **Summer (June - August):** The summer season in Switzerland is perfect for hiking, biking, and exploring the country's many lakes and mountains. The climate is warm and sunny, providing ample opportunities to partake in outdoor recreational activities.

- Fall (September - November): Autumn in Switzerland is characterized by mild weather, colorful foliage, and a variety of cultural events and festivals. It's a great time to visit if you want to enjoy the beauty of Switzerland without the crowds of summer.

Switzerland is a year-round destination with something to offer visitors in every season. However, keep in mind that prices may be higher during peak tourist season, so plan accordingly.

Where to Stay

Switzerland has a variety of accommodation options to suit all tastes and budgets, from budget-friendly hostels to luxurious hotels. Here are some suggestions on where to stay in Switzerland:

1. **Zurich:** As Switzerland's largest city, Zurich offers a wide range of accommodation options, including upscale hotels, boutique hotels, and budget-friendly hostels. The city center is a popular area to stay, with easy access to attractions such as the Swiss National Museum and the Bahnhofstrasse shopping street.

2. **Geneva:** Geneva is another popular city for visitors to Switzerland, with a variety of accommodation options ranging from luxury hotels to budget-friendly hostels. The Old Town area is a great place to stay, with plenty of charm and character.

3. **Interlaken**: Located in the heart of the Swiss Alps, Interlaken is a popular destination for outdoor enthusiasts.

There are a variety of accommodation options in the area, including hotels, hostels, and apartments, with many offering stunning mountain views.

4. **Lucerne:** With its picturesque waterfront and stunning mountain views, Lucerne is a popular destination for visitors to Switzerland. The city offers a range of accommodation options, including upscale hotels, mid-range hotels, and budget-friendly hostels.

5. **Zermatt:** Zermatt is a car-free town nestled in the Swiss Alps, famous for its iconic Matterhorn peak. Visitors can choose from a range of accommodation options, including luxury hotels, mid-range hotels, and cozy mountain chalets.

These are just a few of the many places to stay in Switzerland. When planning your trip, consider your budget, interests, and preferred location to find the perfect accommodation for your needs.

Getting Around

Switzerland has an efficient and reliable public transportation system, making it easy to get around the country. Here are some of the best ways to travel around Switzerland:

1. **Train:** Switzerland boasts an extensive train system that links all significant cities and towns together. Trains run frequently and are generally on time, making them a great way to travel between

destinations. You can purchase tickets at train stations or online.

2. **Bus:** Buses are a great way to get around smaller towns and villages that are not serviced by trains. They also offer scenic routes through the countryside.

3. **Tram and Metro:** Major cities like Zurich and Geneva have extensive tram and metro systems that make it easy to get around the city. These systems are also very affordable.

4. **Car:** If you want more flexibility in your travels, you can rent a car. Keep in mind that Switzerland has narrow and winding roads, and driving can be challenging in mountainous areas. You'll also need a vignette (toll sticker) to drive on highways.

5. **Bike:** Switzerland has an extensive network of bike paths, making it a great place to explore by bike. You can rent bikes at various locations throughout the country.

When traveling around Switzerland, be sure to take advantage of the Swiss Travel Pass, which gives you unlimited travel on trains, buses, and boats, as well as free entry to many museums and attractions.

Conclusion

As your journey to the Swiss Riviera comes to an end, you'll find yourself filled with unforgettable memories of the stunning Lake Geneva, charming towns like Montreux and Vevey, and the rich history and culture of the region. From exploring the Chateau de Chillon and the Charlie Chaplin Museum to indulging in the local cuisine and enjoying lakeside walks, the Swiss Riviera has something to offer everyone.

Whether you're a nature lover, a history buff, a foodie, or simply seeking a peaceful getaway, the Swiss Riviera is the perfect destination. With its breathtaking scenery, rich culture, and warm hospitality, it's no wonder that the region has captured the hearts of travelers from around the world.

So pack your bags, book your tickets, and get ready to experience the magic of the Swiss Riviera for yourself. Your adventure awaits!

Recommendations to optimize your travel experience.

If you're planning a trip to the Swiss Riviera, here are some tips to help you make the most of your experience:

1. **Plan:** Research the attractions and activities you want to experience and plan your itinerary accordingly. By following this, you can maximize your time in the area.

2. **Pack appropriately:** Be sure to bring comfortable walking shoes, as well as clothing that's suitable for the weather. If you're visiting in the summer, don't forget to bring sunscreen and a hat.

3. **Try the local cuisine:** The Swiss Riviera is known for its delicious cuisine, so be sure to try some local specialties like fondue, raclette, and chocolate.

4. **Use public transportation:** Switzerland has an excellent public transportation system, so take advantage of trains, buses, and boats to get around the region. Consider purchasing a Swiss Travel Pass for unlimited travel.

5. **Take in the scenery:** The Swiss Riviera is known for its stunning scenery, so be sure to take time to appreciate the natural beauty of the region. Take a leisurely lakeside walk, hike in the mountains, or simply sit back and enjoy the view.

By following these tips, you'll be well on your way to having an unforgettable trip to the Swiss Riviera.

Printed in Great Britain
by Amazon